P9-ELW-574

DISGUSTING ANIMAL DINNERS

Flies Eat Poop!

Miriam Coleman

PowerKiDS
press™

New York

Published in 2014 by The Rosen Publishing Group, Inc.
29 East 21st Street, New York, NY 10010

First Edition

Editor: Joanne Randolph
Book Design: Kate Vlachos
Photo Research: Katie Stryker

Photo Credits: Cover, pp. 12–13 Dr. Morley Read/Shutterstock.com; front cover (series title) © iStockphoto.com/lishenjun; back cover graphic -Albachiaraa-/Shutterstock.com; p. 5 Radu Bercan/Shutterstock.com; p. 6 iStockphoto/Thinkstock; p. 7 Sylvie Bouchard/Shutterstock.com; p. 8 claffra/Shutterstock.com; p. 9 Erkki Alvenmod/Shutterstock.com; p. 10 photolinc/Shutterstock.com; p. 11 Jubal Harshaw/Shutterstock.com; p. 14 Leonardo Viti/Shutterstock.com; p. 15 HartmutMorgenthal/Shutterstock.com; p. 16 D. Kucharski K. Kucharska/Shutterstock.com; p. 17 sergyiway/Shutterstock.com; p. 19 Javier_Rejon/Shutterstock.com; p. 20 Melissa E Dockstader/Shutterstock.com; p. 21 Jamie Wilson/Shutterstock.com; p. 22 Serg64/Shutterstock.com.

Library of Congress Cataloging-in-Publication Data

Coleman, Miriam, author.
 Flies eat poop! / by Miriam Coleman. — First edition.
    pages cm. — (Disgusting animal dinners)
 Includes index.
 ISBN 978-1-4777-2885-7 (library) — ISBN 978-1-4777-2972-4 (pbk.) —
ISBN 978-1-4777-3044-7 (6-pack)
 1. Diptera—Juvenile literature. 2. Flies—Juvenile literature. I. Title.
 QL533.2.C65 2014
 595.77—dc23
                          2013022583

Manufactured in the United States of America

CPSIA Compliance Information: Batch #W14PK6: For Further Information contact Rosen Publishing, New York, New York at 1-800-237-9932

CONTENTS

Meet the Fly

Flies might be tiny, but these buzzing little creatures can also be deadly. They spend their time in filthy places, eating poop, garbage, and dead animals. Then they fly around and carry the germs all over. They spread **disease**, and they eat farmers' crops.

Although they can be annoying and disgusting, flies also play a very important role in the **ecosystem**. They help **dispose** of things we don't want around and return waste back into the food chain. Some flies even help spread flower pollen in the same way they spread germs.

Flies have large eyes made up of thousands of tiny lenses. This kind of eye is called a compound eye.

Flies Are Everywhere

Flies are insects that make up the order called Diptera. They can be found everywhere on Earth except the coldest parts of the Arctic and Antarctic.

Flies can often be found around farm animals, such as cows and pigs, and wild animals, too. There is plenty of poop to be found around animals!

Fruit flies are a common kind of fly found in people's homes or around fruit at the market. They like to eat rotting fruit.

There are more flies than any other kind of insect. In fact, 1 in every 10 animals that scientists have named is a type of fly! There are more than 150,000 **species** of flies. More than 16,000 of these species live in North America.

Flies have been around for a very long time. The oldest-known fly fossil is 250 million years old.

Flies in Your House

The fly you probably know best is the housefly. Houseflies most likely originally came from central Asia. Now they live all over the world, wherever people and animals live.

They can be found in every kind of climate and **habitat**. You can find them in the country, the city, the forest, or at the beach. Flies especially like to live around farms, where there is plenty of animal **manure**.

Houseflies are common in houses, which gives them their name. However, most houseflies never actually make it inside a house.

If you have ever had a housefly in your house, you know they can be pests. They are noisy as they fly around, and, even worse, they can make you sick by landing on your food.

They also like garbage dumps and houses where they can find lots of kitchen waste. Other common species of flies you might know are mosquitoes, gnats, midges, and blackflies.

The Wings of a Fly

The thing that makes flies different from all other insects is their wings. The name Diptera comes from the Greek words for "two wings." Flies just have one real pair of wings for flying. Where many other insects have a second pair, flies have only small stubs, called halteres, which they use for balance.

Here you can see a close-up of a fly's wings. Do you see that white oval under the main wing? That is one of the halteres.

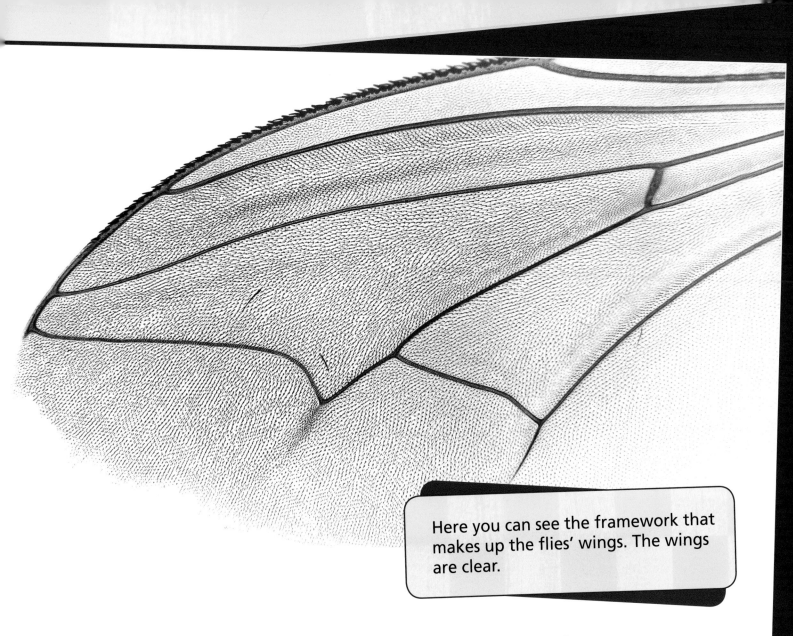

Here you can see the framework that makes up the flies' wings. The wings are clear.

Flies are champions at flying. They can fly forwards, backwards, and upside down and even just hover in place. They can beat their wings faster than any other animal. A housefly beats its wings about 200 times per second.

DISGUSTING FLY FACTS!

1 Fly bodies are covered in tiny scales and hairs, which collect germs wherever they land.

2 A single fly can carry more than 3.5 million bacteria.

3 Flies are able to taste things with the tiny hairs on their feet, so they taste whatever they walk on. If they walk over something that tastes good, they put their mouths down on it to taste it more.

4 Flies often poop while they eat, spreading even more germs.

5 Flies often lay their eggs inside dead animals or even people. When the eggs hatch, the **corpse** is filled with thousands of maggots, which eat the **decaying** flesh.

6 Flesh flies eat nothing but rotting meat.

13

Fly Life Cycle

Female houseflies lay their eggs in places, such as on animal poop or garbage, that will make good food for the young when they hatch. They can lay up to 150 eggs at a time.

Within a day, the eggs hatch into baby flies called maggots. Maggots are larvae. They look like tiny white worms, with no legs or wings.

Maggots are not picky eaters. They will eat garbage, poop, dead animals, and all sorts of disgusting things.

This is an adult robber fly eating a hoverfly. Robber flies tend to live longer than houseflies. Some can live from one to three years.

Over the next week, the maggots eat and grow. When they are big enough, they **inflate** their skin to create a protective case. While inside it, their bodies change and grow wings. This is the pupal stage. Between four and six days later, adult flies break out of the case. The adults can live up to 25 days.

Bug Juice

Adult houseflies can eat only liquid because they have no teeth or jaws to bite and chew up food. Instead, a fly has a long tube called a **proboscis** that comes out of the bottom of its head. On the end of the proboscis is a soft, spongy mouth that the fly can use to suck up or slurp its food.

Here you can see a close-up of this fly's eyes and mouth.

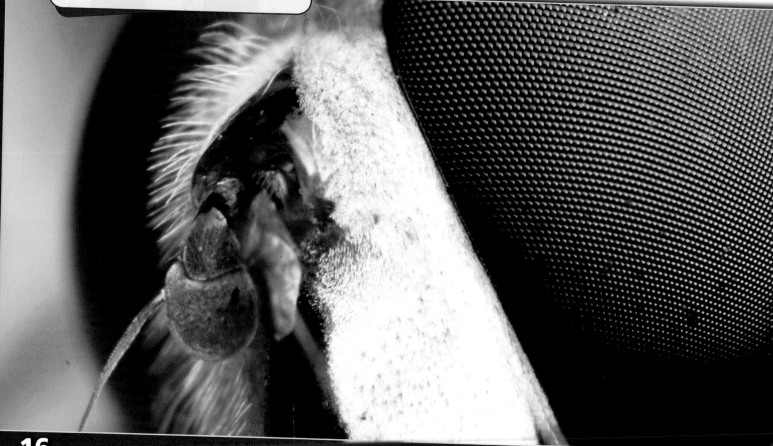

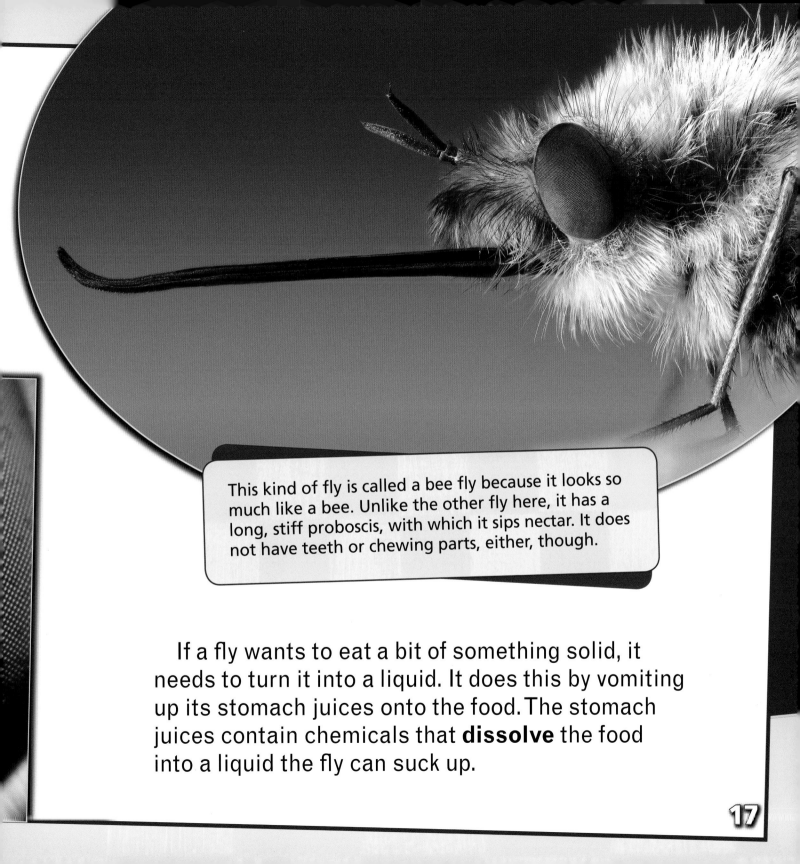

This kind of fly is called a bee fly because it looks so much like a bee. Unlike the other fly here, it has a long, stiff proboscis, with which it sips nectar. It does not have teeth or chewing parts, either, though.

If a fly wants to eat a bit of something solid, it needs to turn it into a liquid. It does this by vomiting up its stomach juices onto the food. The stomach juices contain chemicals that **dissolve** the food into a liquid the fly can suck up.

Why Poop?

For people, **feces** is the worst thing anyone can imagine eating. After all, poop is what our bodies release when we've gotten all the good and useful **nutrients** out of food. Some **protein** and plenty of bacteria are left behind, however, and poop-eating animals, such as flies and dung beetles, have **adapted** to make a meal out of these leftovers. Fresh poop is also soft, so flies can suck it up easily.

Flies also love poop because it offers a nice warm, moist place to lay their eggs. When the eggs hatch, the babies are surrounded by food they can eat.

Some flies were quick to find this fresh waste from a dog in someone's yard.

Other Disgusting Fly Dinners

Flies are most famous for eating poop, but they eat a lot of other disgusting things, too. They love garbage full of old meat and rotting vegetables that turn to liquid as they **ferment**. Maggots eat the decaying flesh of dead animals and even dead people.

There are often many flies around piles of garbage. They like to eat the rotting vegetables and meats.

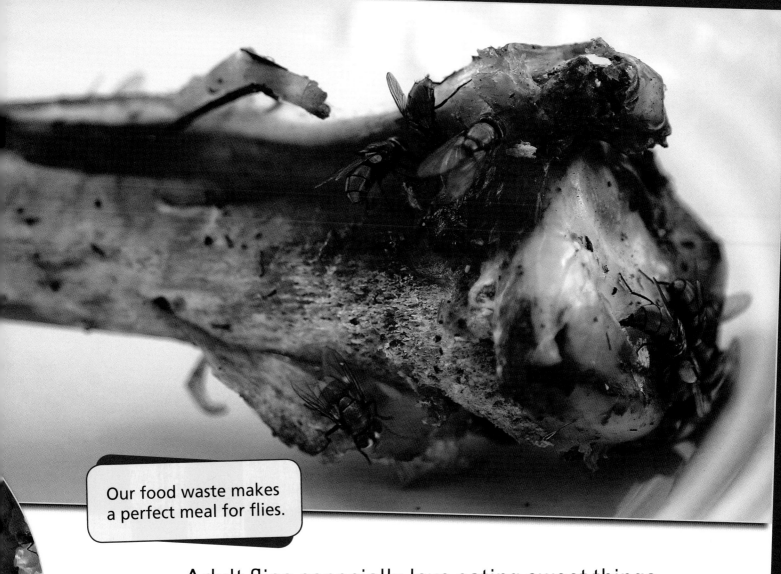

Our food waste makes a perfect meal for flies.

Adult flies especially love eating sweet things, like rotting fruit or even table sugar. Perhaps one of the most disgusting things a fly can do, however, is eat your food. Since flies like to eat pretty much everything, they will often land on your food to eat it, spreading around the germs from all the other disgusting things they have eaten.

Just Doing Their Job

Flies can be pests, spreading germs and disease wherever they go. Knowing what they eat and where their feet have been, you want to be extra careful that they don't land on your food.

Flies are also a useful part of our world. By eating the food nobody else wants, flies help break down waste so that piles of poop and dead animals aren't lying around everywhere. When they eat these disgusting things, they help turn them into soil as they pass through their bodies. Although they can seem disgusting and unpleasant to us, these animals have an important job to do.

Flies are disgusting, but as with all animals, they have a part to play in our ecosystem. They get rid of stuff we do not want and feed many animals, such as birds.

GLOSSARY

adapted (uh-DAPT-ed) Changed to fit new conditions.

corpse (KORPS) A dead body.

decaying (dih-KAY-ing) Rotting.

disease (dih-ZEEZ) An illness or sickness.

dispose (dih-SPOHZ) To get rid of something.

dissolve (dih-ZOLV) To break down.

ecosystem (EE-koh-sis-tem) A community of living things and the surroundings in which they live.

feces (FEE-seez) The solid waste of animals.

ferment (fur-MENT) To change in a way that makes gas bubbles.

habitat (HA-buh-tat) The surroundings where an animal or a plant naturally lives.

inflate (in-FLAYT) To fill with air.

manure (muh-NUHR) Animal waste that is used on farms to help crops grow.

nutrients (NOO-tree-unts) Food that a living thing needs to live and grow.

proboscis (pruh-BAH-sus) A tubelike mouthpart that insects use to suck in liquid food.

protein (PROH-teen) An important element inside the cells of plants and animals.

species (SPEE-sheez) A single kind of living thing. All people are one species.

INDEX

WEBSITES

Due to the changing nature of Internet links, PowerKids Press has developed an online list of websites related to the subject of this book. This site is updated regularly. Please use this link to access the list: www.powerkidslinks.com/dad/flies/